Did I Say That?

How to Communicate in Everyday Life

Linda Seatts

Copyright © 2012 Linda Seatts

All rights reserved.

ISBN: 0979330513
ISBN-13:978-0-9793305-1-3

DEDICATION

To my late parents, Lowell and Lillian Massey who taught me that everything is within your reach, just work hard, do your best, have faith and stand strong. To my only son, Anthony, whose faith and obedience to his mother and father allowed me to concentrate on my dreams.

CONTENTS

	Acknowledgements	1
1	Introduction	2
2	What is Communication?	11
3	Different Perspectives: Avoiding the Conflict	25
4	Modus Operandi (MO): You Should Know me by Now	38
5	Did I Say That? Interpreting the Message	43
6	Expectations	57
7	Wisdom: When to respond and when to Ignore	61
8	Making It Work	66

ACKNOWLEDGMENTS

I wish to thank and acknowledge Timeka N. Williams, Doctoral Candidate, Instructor, and Researcher in Communication Studies, at the University of Michigan, Ann Arbor, for taking the time out of her busy schedule to review and edit this manuscript.

1 INTRODUCTION

One of the easiest things to do is communicate—to talk, exchange ideas, perspectives and points of views. However, it wasn't until I entered the workforce, and later study conflict resolution, that I realized communication is easy but it's the interpretation that causes nations to go to war, relationships to end, and otherwise qualified workers to lose their jobs.

There are people right now who left a job because of a misunderstanding that perhaps could have been resolved with a conversation.

There are brothers and sisters, fathers and sons, mothers and daughters that are not talking to one another because of the way someone interpreted an innocent comment or conversation.

In my over 25 years of teaching and counseling, I've encountered married couples who are on the verge of a separation or divorce because of misunderstood communication and/or no communication.

There are hundreds of books on communication that focus on specific areas such as gender, ethnicity, lifestyle, class, etc., however, this easy-to-read book focuses on everyday people, real life situations and interactions.

In just 70 short pages, you'll gain the tools necessary to interpret all types of communication accurately. This in turn, should help you avoid troubled relationships and other life issues that result from misunderstood communication.

Most importantly I hope that after reading this book you will be empowered to mend a broken relationship(s) that was destroyed through a series of misunderstandings. You may realize that telling the other person what *really* hurt your feelings (in a way that he or she can easily understand) could bridge the gap that was created when you first stopped communicating.

Before we cut off relationships we should at least give the individual(s) an opportunity to explain why they said what they said, because nine times out of ten it was something you or the other individual(s) misinterpreted.

I hope this book will help you avoid conflict by taking the time to understand the point of view of the messenger and to acknowledge your own method of thinking that may be the cause of the miscommunication.

Although conflict is unavoidable and we will have to face conflict in life, creating conflict through misunderstandings is something we can avoid.

Through research and careful reflection I realized that one root cause of failed communication is the fact that we tend to put more expectations on others than ourselves. Expectations of others are also often silent and never get discussed until after a conflict has already occurred. I am not saying expectations are negative, because we should have expectations of our spouse, children and employees and anyone else we find ourselves in relationship with, but expectations should only be placed if you have told the other individual(s).

Over and over again, we place so many non-communicated expectations on other people and "expect" a person to react in a certain way. Once you place an expectation on someone and it's not met, conflict enters and disagreements are birthed. How can you place expectations on someone without letting them know your expectations?

Everybody is different, and once we realize the personality of an individual, and how they react—why do we keep trying to make them react the way we want? We cannot control the thoughts of other adults—but we can try to take the time to understand how they process and interpret information.

In the process of placing expectations on others, we often become disengaged from any real self-evaluation. In the midst of a misunderstanding or mis-communication, we are apt to point the finger at someone else rather than looking within.

Why is it that when we hear motivational talks, even spiritual sermons that identify human faults and other personal issues, we immediately think that the speaker is talking about someone *else*?

I will never forget what my late mother, Lillian Massey a great mother and woman of wisdom, would constantly communicate to me and my siblings, *"whenever you are in a dispute, look within—and you will find something."* I use her advice and it works. I always found if I wasn't a contributor to the conflict, I certainly could make an honest and forthright attempt to resolve the conflict.

I have conducted diversity workshops throughout the country and have worked with people from over 100 countries and over the years continue to witness simple misunderstandings that could be avoided if people would step outside of themselves and try to truly understand the intended message—the story behind the message and the perspective/point of view of the one talking.

I have also interacted with people who take no regard for the other person and just "spout off." On a personal note, I use to believe it's better to be honest and to the point instead of "sugar-coating" the message; and once again, my mother would tell me *"it's not what I am saying it's how I am saying it."* She said I should give the message but in a gentler manner and again she was right.

In this fast-paced society—fueled by instant messages, texting, blogs, Twitter, Facebook, and Smartphones, we are always moving quickly--running to pick up the kids, cook dinner, get to work, places of worship, etc., and because of our busy lives we are mentally and physically drained. This fatigue triggers us to "jump" to conclusions without truly understanding and processing the words that have been spoken or received.

I hope you will take the time to read this book and most importantly, be honest. If you think you are perfect and you know everything, or if you are the type of person who is looking for growth, to build your character and healthy relationships, this book is for you. I look forward to hearing your feedback at *lindaseatts@gmail.com* or on twitter at *@DidISayThatHow?*

2 WHAT IS COMMUNICATION?

1a: a process by which information is exchanged between individuals through a common system of symbols, signs, or behavior[1]

Communication is two-way—and it's free. We have the ability to talk to one another and exchange information. Free speech is a blessing. There are many people in other countries that fight and lose their life to speak freely.

While growing up, I could not understand why my family didn't talk about certain things. I also wondered why people who were upset

---

Merriam Webster On-line Dictionary, www.meriam-webster.com.

with each other would not try to sit down and work it out; only if it was that easy! As I grew up I realized conversations were more productive when one person in the communication exchange took the time to really hear between the lines of what the other person was really trying to say, "the story behind the story."

As I will share with you in the following pages—sometimes when two people are in a heated exchange of words, it's best for one person to just be quiet—to defuse the situation. Conceding or just deciding to stop going back and forth in an exchange of heated words, **<u>doesn't mean you agree with the other person</u>**—it means that you are willing to lead the exchange and stop the communication until people cool down. Conceding shows that you are the bigger person and you realize that continuous exchanges will only escalate to more anger.

Honey What's Wrong?

Let's imagine a real life example: a wife asks her husband to pick up her clothes from the cleaners because she has to work late and he says okay. Unfortunately, the husband got caught in a traffic jam because of a bad accident. When he arrived home without the clothes he said, *"I am sorry, I wasn't able to make it."* The wife gets upset, *"what do you mean you didn't make it…..I can't believe you couldn't do something as simple as ……..?"* Her husband could have avoided this had he included the reason why he didn't fulfill his obligation; here's a better answer: *"Honey, I am so sorry, there was an accident and I got stuck in traffic."* To take it a step further, if he had a cell phone he should have called her while stuck in traffic and perhaps another arrangement could be made.

Many times the important details left out of the communication leads to conflict. For some reason we expect the other person to fill in the details of the conversation.

The Workplace

One of the reasons people don't communicate is because they anticipate a certain outcome.

For example, Diane was coordinating a bi-weekly event at work and found out at the last minute that the location was being renovated. She didn't tell her boss because she was trying to work it out herself. However, it never worked out and because she didn't tell her boss, it turned into a negative outcome where folks showed up and the event was cancelled.

While trying to prove she could handle things on her own, Diane ended up making things worse. She had been told in the past to give her boss an update if there were any problems or changes.

The time her boss and other staff members wasted answering phone calls and organizing for the event could have been avoided with a simple communication to her boss like this, *"Edward, just an FYI, I was just told that the Blake room is undergoing some renovation and it might not be ready for this week's event—I should have a definitive answer by tomorrow afternoon."* Short, simple and free! Bosses have a way of finding out anyway, so why not demonstrate leadership skills to your boss by communicating.

Classroom Projects—Students Speak Up

The poor communication habits that we exhibit as adults, are often leftover from childhood. Young people need help communicating too, especially in school. Imagine this scenario: you are working on a class project and you are responsible for writing a summary page of the research project for your team.

Something came up and you won't have your assignment ready for your next class meeting. You are hesitant to let your teammates know because you **anticipate** they might get upset. In the hopes of avoiding an uncomfortable conversation, you show up at class unprepared, and now they are *really* upset. One of your classmates asks, *"why didn't you text us or email us that you didn't have your part done? We could have helped you."*

The refusal to communicate made a small problem worse.

There are so many examples of reasons why people hesitate to communicate and later find out they worried for no reason.

There have been times when I lost sleep over how I thought someone might react to some type of exchange but when I communicated the information they reacted totally opposite of what I anticipated.

I am thankful that now I don't worry anymore as I have learned over the years, *"don't sweat the small stuff."*

Body Language Speaks Louder than Words

There are other non-verbal "symbols" that communicate strong messages without a word leaving a person's mouth. For example, have you ever walked into a place of business and someone is sitting behind a desk with their arms folded and head tilted to the side? Without them saying a word their body language says, *"and what do you want because I don't feel like being bothered."*

Dr. Albert Mehrabian, best known for his work in the field of non-verbal communication (body language) suggests that body language is the major expression of messages.

Many people don't realize that active listening is communication. His research also indicates that non-verbal communications and/or body language account for up to 93% of the meaning that people take from any human communication.

Body language is the most common, and strongest form of communication.

It is incredible what a smile can do—a smile can defuse a tense situation and, a smile can bring out the best in a person.

When you are conversing with someone behind a desk, leaning forward with your arms resting on the table and clasping your hands, communicates you are interested in what someone is saying.

Eye contact communicates interest with an occasional nod of the head which means, *"I hear what you are saying."* However, when a person is nodding their head while you are talking doesn't necessarily mean they agree with what you are saying, it just acknowledges that they hear what you are saying.

When you are communicating with

someone with your head down or looking away, raises red flags of dishonesty, even though that might not be the case. Eye contact communicates strength, confidence and truth. On the other hand, just because a person is looking you straight in the eyes while they are talking is not an indication they are telling the truth—don't you love oxymorons?

Below are some examples of interpreting Body Language

Body Language	Meaning
Looking right	Lying and/or guessing
Frequent Blinking	Excitement
One arm clasping the other by your side	Nervousness and/or defensiveness
Touching or scratching	Lying and/or exaggeration

nose while speaking	
Ear Tugging	Indecision
Neck Scratching	Disbelief
Running hands through hair	Flirting
Leg Position when sitting	Interest if knees are pointed towards you and disinterest if knees are pointed away.

Oops!—I Didn't ignore you on Purpose

One of the biggest mistakes we make is how we interpret body language. For example, have you ever been in deep thought about something and realized that you walked by someone you know and didn't speak? The person you passed knows you well and knows that you normally speak. You didn't mean any harm you were just engrossed in thinking about something that was heavy on your mind; I call it being "in a zone."

That person, hopefully, will not interpret your non-communication as being rude. However, you know when that happens to you, there are times you may say to yourself or others, *"I saw Brenda and she walked right by me and didn't speak."* We should follow-up with, *"she probably has a lot on her mind,"* especially if you know Brenda is a friendly individual.

The point here is not to always assume someone is being rude if they don't speak, especially if you know the personality and character of the individual.

It's important for us to be mindful of how we are communicating both verbally and nonverbally.

Key Points

1) Don't anticipate or assume an outcome if you are not 100% sure. Ninety-nine percent of the time, the outcome you anticipated is wrong. It's better to communicate sooner than later.
2) Talk—it's free!
3) Just because you decide to be calm and perhaps silent, during a conversation, does not mean you agree with the person. On the contrary, you have decided to take a leadership role and allow the situation to cool down.
4) Don't always assume someone is being rude if they don't speak to you, especially if you know the personality and character of the individual. In fact, ask the person if everything is okay.

5) Remember we all get tired at some point and time so avoid quickly jumping to conclusions without getting the facts directly from the source.

3 DIFFERENT PERSPECTIVES: AVOIDING CONFLICT

Perspective (Point of view)
2a: the interrelation in which a subject or its parts are mentally viewed <places the issues in proper perspective>; also: POINT OF VIEW b: the capacity to view things in their true relations or relative importance <trying to maintain my perspective>
2

I used to be a very opinionated individual. It was either my way or no way, and with that kind of attitude, my future opportunities for success was limited. An opinionated person is someone you try to avoid having meaningful conversations with, especially on

---

Merriam Webster On-line Dictionary, www.meriam-webster.com.

"controversial" subjects such as religion and politics. However, if you live with someone who is opinionated, or if that person is you, communication is probably inevitable. So how do you deal with an opinionated individual(s)?

Agree to Disagree

First, we must understand that in this wonderful United States of America, we have the luxury of "free speech" something that many people from other countries are losing their lives to obtain. We have to remember that although you don't agree with an individual's perspective or point of view doesn't mean you have to dislike the person, it means you dislike their opinion. Because you dislike their opinion doesn't mean you end a relationship.

Now let's put this in perspective—this does, of course, depend on the opinion. I am not talking about extremist opinions such as racist views or someone who advocates domestic violence—these are not opinions they are dangerous expressions of hatred. I am talking about, everyday normal interactions. Domestic violence and hatred isn't normal behavior.

For example, you have a friend who wants to home school their children, and you feel that children need to be exposed to other kids for a healthy socialization process. Because you both disagree with each other's point of view does not mean that either one of you is wrong, you just hold different opinions. Is a difference of opinion worth losing a friendship or relationship?

When I started listening to people with

whom I disagreed, I was able to get another perspective, which broadened my understanding of the topic and increased my knowledge and intellect. Although I may still disagree I have a better understanding of the subject.

For example, I used to believe in capital punishment and got into some rather "lively" discussions on this topic. But after hearing the other person's perspective I actually changed my view. Unfortunately, we have more talkers than listeners. If talkers would listen more closely, they may gain better insight into the issue discussed.

Have you ever had a conversation with someone and they constantly confirm they heard you but you know they didn't because ten minutes later they didn't do what you thought they heard you asked them to do?

Active listening is something we all need to work on daily—to focus on what the other person is saying – giving them 100% attention. What is active listening? Active listening is when you make a conscious effort to hear not only the words that another person is saying but, more importantly, try to understand the complete message being communicated. The first step is called:

Attending to the person you are talking to using eye contact, posture and gestures. Earlier we talked about the importance of non-verbal symbols and the importance of facing the person, opening your posture, leaning towards the individual, eye contact and relaxing while attending to the individual(s). The second step is called:

Paraphrasing rather than assuming you are receiving the words correctly you restate the message in fewer words. For example, Marla came to you and said, *"Johnny, I don't know what's wrong with Craig—he does not want to participate in the teambuilding event."* You paraphrase by saying, *"So I am hearing that Craig doesn't want to participate in the event, did you ask him why?"* Marla responded, *"Yes—because of the $5 contribution we all have to make for the lunch—he doesn't want to contribute financially to the food, and will be bringing his own lunch."* Johnny explains, *"Well let Craig know not to worry about the $5.00, he can bring his own lunch to the event, because I am expecting everyone to participate."*

Do you see how Johnny made sure he clearly understood by paraphrasing what Marla told him and he even asked her a question—he didn't want to assume anything. On the other hand if Marla or Johnny were not empathetic, they could have accepted Craig's resistance which may have led to conflict, resentment and damage to the team.

When we are actively listening, we must:

Put the other person at ease. Give them space, and time, and "permission" to speak. When we actively listen we should be:

Clarifying what they said, put it in sharper focus. You are at this time confirming that you understand what they are saying while also helping them see another point of view. For example, someone tells you, *"I am so tired of all of the changes around here—I can't finish anything."* You would clarify this statement by saying, *"So you are overwhelmed with a lot of work?"* You see, active listening determines the real issue. The issue in this conversation is not that the individual dislikes changes—the real issue is she is overwhelmed with work.

Summarizing is pulling together, organizing, and integrating the major aspects of your dialogue. **Pay attention to** various themes and emotional overtones. Put key ideas and feelings into broad statements. **DO NOT** add new ideas.

For example, you may have experienced having a rather long, detailed conversation with someone and when you bring up the topic an hour later, you find out that half of what you said wasn't comprehended. If there are certain people that this happens with consistently, you should try summarizing the conversation, then ask, *"are we clear?"*

All of the steps we have discussed thus far should be incorporated in each and every conversation—including:

Empathy which is the ability to imagine oneself in another's place and understand the other's feelings, desires, ideas, and action. This is something we all need to remember and practice.

Showing empathy in a conversation conveys to the person that you are listening and you understand their experience--even though you yourself may not have personally experienced it, you can put yourself in their shoes. For example, Elizabeth calls Kara to tell her that her husband Harold is leaving her. Elizabeth has two kids and is a stay-at-home mom. Kara is an Administrator for a large health system making six figures and does not have any kids.

Showing empathy, Kara tells her friend: *"Elizabeth, I am so sorry about this—I know this is hard for you and you know I am here for you. How can I help you?"* She displayed empathy by acknowledging that this is a painful experience. Although Kara has never been in this situation, she puts herself into her friend's shoes and recognizes that she's in a hard place.

A classic example is the story of a mom who finds her children, Jerry and Sandra quarreling over an orange they both want. She grabs the orange, cuts it in half, and both children break out crying. It turns out Sandra wanted the whole peel, in one continuous cut, for a school project. Jerry wanted the juice of an entire orange, for a cake he promised to bake for his best friend's birthday.

Had the mother stopped and asked her children why they were quarrelling over the orange the conflict could have been solved. This is an example of daily interactions that lead to conflict because people decided not to "communicate," and based their actions on assumptions.

Imagine this scenario: you present an idea to your boss—and your boss expresses that it's a good idea, but cannot implement it at this time. Because you were passionate about your idea, you become upset with your boss' response. Your boss, on the other hand has a boss who has a strategic focus and more in-depth knowledge of the vision of the office and where she wants it to go. Your boss also has to answer to someone and perhaps your idea is something that has already been considered.

If you are a manager and someone brings an idea to you, it is helpful to explain why the idea was turned down. That way you are avoiding guessing games from your employee. The employee might still be upset, but at least you have explained the reason.

By offering details and explanations in our communication, we offer the other person the "story behind the story" and tend to avoid conflict.

Key Points

1) Active listening is key in understanding what a person is trying to communicate. Reading between the lines, (what is the person really saying?) is key to effective communication. Listening may change

your perspective on a subject.

2) Understanding a person's point of view doesn't mean you agree.

3) Take the time to stop and understand the purpose of the conversation.

4) Be empathetic.

5) Avoid conflict by offering "the story behind the story" when you communicate.

4 MODUS OPERANDI (MO): YOU SHOULD KNOW ME BY NOW

***MO:** a method of procedure; especially : a distinct pattern or method of operation.*[3]

I remember having rich discussions with my late sister, Lois, who used to work in the sex crimes unit for an urban police department. She would talk to me about the perils of the police department. When I asked her questions about her job or gave suggestions, she would get very "passionate and emotional" about it. Rightly so, because she was there, she knew what was going on, she was on the front-line exhausting her

---

[3] Ibid.

mental and physical energies. After subsequent conversations I realized that she just needed someone to listen. What led to my conclusion that my sister needed a listener? It was her MO—her pattern of operation. She was very passionate about her job, especially her empathy for the victims. When she talked about her day and the challenges at work, it wasn't for feedback, she was venting, and needed a listening ear.

More MO's

Why would you continue to tell your personal business to a known gossiper then later complain that your business was spread around?

Why would you continue to expect someone to pay you back when you lent them money in the past and they never pay you back? You have an expectation that has never been met and for some reason you think this person has changed overnight.

Once you know where a person is coming from, their MO, it's easier to communicate with them. If you know what makes a person upset—why push their buttons?

For example, Sara's best friend Tinsley doesn't like Sara's husband Jim. Jim isn't perfect, but he is a kind and devoted husband. Whenever Sara had a disagreement with Jim, she would tell Tinsley and Tinsley would always say negative things about Jim to Sara. Sara would get upset with Tinsley because she "expected" Tinsley to give sound advice rather than negative comments.

The definition of insanity is doing the same thing and expecting a different result. If this is Tinsley's MO, then why does Sara have different expectations? Don't talk to Tinsley about problems in your marriage--change the conversation and talk to someone who will give you wise counsel.

Another common mistake people make in in communicating is seeking advice from folks who are doing the same thing they are doing, folks who don't know any more than the person asking questions. When you want wisdom—some objective advice—you need to go to an individual you know will tell you the truth whether you like it or not.

You want to talk to people who are objective not subjective. Objective people will look at all points of view and give you honest feedback that may not agree with your view of the situation. Subjective people will give you advice that may agree with you or sabotage you.

Key Points

1) Identify a person's MO and interact accordingly.

2) Listen to wise counsel—someone who will tell you the truth rather it hurts you or not. Stop expecting different feedback from a person that always gives you the same feedback every time you talk about a subject. Remember you can't change an adult—unless they want to change.

3) Insanity is doing the same thing, and expecting a different result.

5 DID I SAY THAT? INTERPRETING THE MESSAGE?

Interpretation
1: to explain or tell the meaning of : present in understandable terms <interpret dreams>[4]

Conflict intersects with interpretation. Merriam-Webster defines interpretation as the explanation or telling the meaning. For example, Gerald is notorious for being late even though he says he will be there in five minutes. Jasmine just met Gerald and they were going on their first date. He called her and said he would be at her house in five minutes, but five minutes turned into Gerald's

---
[4] Ibid.

normal 30 to 60 minutes late. Because Jasmine doesn't know Gerald's "MO," when he showed up she was upset and the date ended before it even began. Gerald is so used to his own tardiness, he could not understand why Jasmine was upset.

Jasmine interpreted his words literally, "I will be there in five minutes." Jasmine is a punctual individual who is always on time. She interpreted his message from her frame of reference because she is honest, and keeps her word. So, Gerald had a rude awakening on the phrase, "mean what you say and say what you mean."

Here's another example of interpretation gone wrong: James, a manager of the sales group of an Engineering firm, interpreted his bosses comment in a meeting as a personal attack. James' boss, Andrew, said to the group *"we have to do better in supporting our sales team."* James interpreted this communication as a personal attack on his leadership. However, when Andrew said, "we" he really meant the entire firm needs to provide better financial support and incentives for the entire sales team. Andrew knew what his words meant, but James interpreted it from his point of view as a loyal, and hard-working manager.

How would James know that Andrew wasn't attacking him? Because James is an advocate of communication he asked to have a meeting with his boss and expressed his concern over the comment. It was during this conversation that Andrew explained that he wasn't talking about James but about the firm as a whole. Andrew explained that because the firm is so focused on their products and services, they don't give enough attention to the sales team.

We tend to interpret words and images from our frame of reference, our view, our lens. For example, look at the image below—what is it?

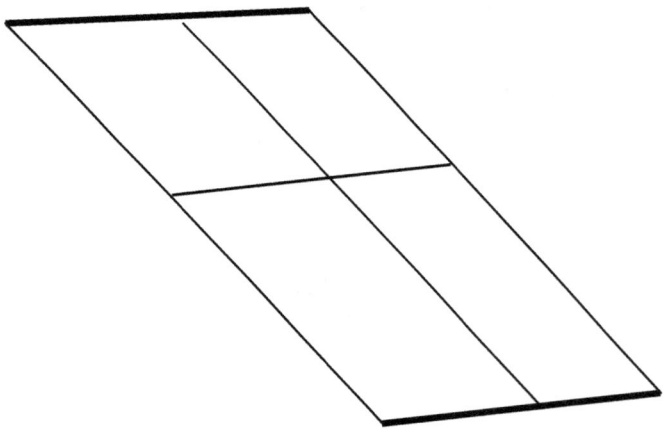

There is no right or wrong answer. What you see will depend on your lens, your worldview, your perspective.

Some see a cross, a window, a tennis court, what do you see?

This is an example of how we communicate. We start off with our own views, personalities and perspectives and we begin a conversation. Somebody is talking from the view of the window, the other the tennis court and all you are trying to do is talk about the cross! This image shows how our words are interpreted when we are communicating from unique perspectives.

For example, two kids ages 12 and 9 were told by their mother to learn how to catch the bus. She told them to *stand* at the bus stop. The two children walked to the bus stop but when they got there they noticed the Bus Stop sign and at the top read, "No Standing." So the two were confused and thought they were not supposed to stand there. They walked to another bus stop and again the sign said "No Standing." After trying a third sign only to see the "No Standing" sign again, they gave up and walked to their grandparents house where they got in trouble. But the children were simply interpreting what they thought was a rule that forbid them from standing at a bus stop. Do you see how different interpretations lead to different results?

Here's another example: I told my son to clean up the counter that was filled with pots and bowls as I just completed preparing a salad and meat for the grill. My interpretation of cleaning up the counter was to clean it up and wash the dishes that were on the counter. My son's interpretation of "clean up the counter" was to clear the counter by wiping it and placing the pots and pans in the sink. When I walked in the kitchen I said to him, *"I thought I told you to clean up the counter."* He responded, *"I did—I didn't know you meant for me to wash the dishes too."*

Interpreting communication from two different perspectives causes conflict and misunderstandings. The messenger, or communicator, has in their mind an expectation within their view and perspective. This expectation is simply an assumption of how the other person will respond to the message, and causes a misunderstanding when that assumption proves false. You cannot assume that people can read your mind or know what you want, but you can communicate exactly what you want. You might say, *"well they should know that."* Why should they know that—did you tell them—

are you making an assumption based on your relationship, their gender, and/or position, etc...?

For example, Thomas is used to teasing his wife about her big feet and she laughs along with him. But one day, she gets upset, and Thomas is perplexed and wonders why she is upset today since she always laughed when he joked about this in the past. Thomas asked his wife, *"what happened, why you are upset?"* She responded—*"I am getting tired of you talking about my feet."* All along she didn't like it but she never said anything, and that was a big mistake.

If you put up with joking, or other comments and go along with it that communicates that you agree or approve of the joking. If you don't like something, speak up the first time, *"honey, I am sensitive about my feet—please don't make fun because it hurts me."* That's simple, and free—that is communication!

Today, there are broken relationships because somebody misinterpreted a conversation and/or put up with communication they didn't like but never let the other person know they were offended or hurt by their words.

For example, Jake is laid off from his job, and getting unemployment. He talked to his brother Dennis to get advice on whether he should take a job that is paying $300 a month less than his current unemployment income check. Dennis responded, *"that's only a $300, decrease, you won't be able to stay on unemployment forever."* Jake got upset because $300 is the difference between staying in his home and becoming homeless. Jake thought Dennis was being insensitive. However, Dennis didn't mean to hurt Jake—he was talking from his perspective—because Dennis was employed and was earning enough that if he had to take a monthly decrease of $300 it would not impact his ability to stay in his home. Was Dennis being insensitive? Not really, he was speaking from his perspective.

Do you see how we can misinterpret words?

Many times our current emotional/mental condition and/or mood affects our ability to correctly interpret the meaning of words. If you have low-self-esteem, everything a person says will travel through your mental state of low self-esteem, the same for any other personal issues you may have such as insecurity, sensitivity, etc. For example, a person who is super-sensitive and insecure may interpret a regular conversation or comment as a personal attack.

For example, Rachel has a consistent MO of cutting off relationships for no apparent reason. You can be having fun—hanging out—talking, having a good relationship then the next thing you know, Rachel stops answering your phone calls. You try to figure out why.

Was it something I said, what did I do? The majority of the time, it is an innocent conversation that Rachel misinterpreted through her lens. In other words, she misinterpreted a conversation based on what she is thinking rather it's true or not. The danger here is that Rachel will not talk to the individual to get an understanding. She makes up her mind and will talk when she's ready which can be days, months or years. Because this is Rachel's "MO" you can't take it personal, but it may still be painful.

Do not text or email while you are upset!

In the introduction of this book, I talked about the fast-paced technical world in which we live. The information age is a good age if we work it to our advantage!

The worst thing we can do is send an email or text message in response to a problem, misunderstanding, or other serious dialogue. The rule of thumb is waiting a few hours, even 24 hours to cool off before you respond. Some email and/or text messages are uniquely designed for "voice-to-voice" live conversations, not voicemail, not e-mail, not texting!

For example, I received a very unprofessional, accusatory and inaccurate email from a colleague. I read it—then I decided to wait a few hours before I responded. Since I have dealt with my fair share of unfriendly, unprofessional and non-collegial e-mails, I have learned to become cool, calm and collected when dealing with them. When I responded I didn't "fuel" the anger by responding as unprofessional as he did, I responded professionally stating the facts.

My other rule of thumb regarding technology is to never go back and forth on e-mail or texting—after two times, it's time to have a live telephone conversation. It's easy for people to hide behind e-mail and texting. If you can't say something face-to-face the bottom line is that you shouldn't use e-mail or text messages to say it either. Being mature means owning our communication, regardless of the final outcome--don't say it if you can't take the response!

Key Points

1) Make sure you actively listen before you jump to conclusions. Hearing how the other person received your comments might change the way you react.

2) Don't continue to engage in joking or other comments that you don't like—stand up and let the individual(s) know you don't appreciate the comments and communicate how it makes you feel.

3) Never respond to an email or text when you are upset or tired. Wait a few hours, if you can 24 hours, to give you time to sleep and respond with a fresh mind.

6 EXPECTATIONS

Expectations
4a: to consider probable or certain <expect to be forgiven> <expect that things will improve> b : to consider reasonable, due, or necessary <expected hard work from the students> c : to consider bound in duty or obligated <they expect you to pay your bills>[5]

I briefly talked about this in the previous chapters—but this is so important it deserves more attention. Silent expectations is the center of conflict. We have placed so many expectations on people, and the most interesting part of it all is we never communicated our expectations. We assume

---

[5] Ibid.

when people know us, they are *supposed* to know what we expect from them

How does your husband know that you expect a birthday card on your birthday unless you tell him? How does your son or daughter know what time to come home if you don't tell them? How do you expect your parent(s) to know you need some money unless you ask them?

For example, a manager gave her assistant several projects that were all priority. When her manager gave her yet another project, the assistant *assumed* her boss didn't *expect* her to meet the deadlines of the other projects. However, her assistant never asked her boss, and her boss wasn't pleased the deadlines weren't met. The assistant could have simply communicated to her boss that she needed some assistance with prioritizing. Words are free—but with all of the conflict and misunderstandings that occur every minute of the day, you would think it cost a million dollars per word to speak. From this scenario the assistant was also thinking for her boss. The assistant probably had a mental conversation that went something like this: *"well obviously she knows how much work I have so she can't possibly think I can meet the deadlines."* If the assistant was *thinking* about this—why was it hard for her to communicate her thoughts through her mouth?

Never think for someone else—just ask! Nine times out of ten your thinking for someone else will not be accurate.

It is unfair to everyone when assumptions are made regarding a communication exchange. It's so important to get clarification if you are confused or hurt by the communication. I am not saying that you are going to like everything someone says—just make sure you give them a chance to say it, and that you understand their message clearly.

Key Points:

1) If you place expectations on people, tell them your expectations.
2) Never assume that the other person knows what you want or what they are thinking.
3) If there's any doubt in your understanding, get clarification by asking questions.

7 WISDOM: WHEN TO RESPOND AND WHEN TO IGNORE

Wisdom
1a : accumulated philosophic or scientific learning :
KNOWLEDGE *b : ability to discern inner qualities and relationships :* INSIGHT *c : good sense :* JUDGMENT *d : generally accepted belief <challenges what has become accepted wisdom among many historians — Robert Darnton> 2: a wise attitude, belief, or course of action*
3: the teachings of the ancient wise men[6]

I have written a lot on "how" to communicate. Now I am going to talk about how "not" to communicate. This chapter on wisdom will discuss having the ability to analyze the situation to determine if there is a

---

[6] Ibid.

need to communicate.

Analyzing the situation means looking carefully at the situation. Is the setting a professional or personal environment? Is the person that communicated the message in a power position? Is a response necessary? There is a wise saying, "know what battles to pick." I am not saying that the communication exchange is a battle, but sometimes we just have to let things go—even though it may hurt our feelings.

Secondly, sometimes there has to be a hard conversation. I mean there are times when you have to give some constructive criticism or feedback that no matter how nice and respectful you say it, the other person may not receive it well, and it won't be because there was a mis-communication or mis-understanding. Sometimes honest feedback will not be received with bells and whistles. So I want to make sure you understand that all communication will not be rosy, and may lead to conflict even though you tried hard to avoid it. The truth hurts, but if we allow it, it helps shape our character and integrity. Many of us are familiar with the serenity prayer, *"God grant me the serenity to accept the things I cannot change, the courage to change the things I can and the wisdom to know the difference."*

My hope is that you develop the wisdom to know when to react, respond or ignore. For example, I remember when a friend of mine, Amber was severely struggling financially to take care of her son, and her sister jokingly said, *"you only have one bottle of perfume?"* That really hurt Amber because her sister didn't know how hard Amber was struggling, and the sacrifice Amber made just to have one bottle of perfume, opposed to her sister having 5 or 6 because she was making a lot more money than Amber.

Was her sister being insensitive? No. She was commenting from her perspective--her point of view, her "lens," and Amber interpreted her words as being insensitive. Although it hurt Amber, and this happened over 10 years ago, it wasn't a big enough deal for Amber to react or respond so she **ignored** it. No love was lost—and the relationship didn't suffer over such a minor comment.

Key Points

1) All communication will not be accepted, no matter how nice you say it.

2) Be aware that you will have to determine whether or not to react, respond or ignore a communication exchange.

8 MAKING IT WORK

Now that you have been given all the practical tools to effectively communicate, please remember there will be times when you follow all of the steps outlined in this book and you will still encounter negative responses and conflict. I briefly touched on this in Chapter 3.

There are people you are close to, maybe in your family, that no matter what you say or how nicely you say it your words will be misinterpreted. Why? Often there are deeper issues that require professional and spiritual attention. This book isn't about dealing with people with damaged emotions, but keep in mind that there are many people who are emotionally damaged to the point that it impairs their ability to communicate and interpret communication effectively.

For example, there was a young lady who as a child was constantly teased about her weight and her size. As an adult, she became very self-conscious of words spoken to her and she took everything personally. She had to work through these issues and must continue to work through them. She sought spiritual help through her faith in God.

Unfortunately, there are many people today still suffering from childhood experiences and refuse to acknowledge that pain. As a result of these unhealed wounds, they often misinterpret words and non-verbal symbols as personal attacks against them. My hope is if that person is you, you will seek the help that you need to be free of the past and to accept the beauty of life.

Timing

I touched on this earlier, but I want to stress the importance of timing when communicating. Timing is key! For example, try to avoid serious conversation if you are feeling ill or are exhausted. Also, do not communicate criticism at the wrong time, especially in already stressful situations. For example, the day of an event someone spent months to plan, before a major presentation, etc.

Whenever we enter into dialogue we can apply one of the most popular instructions we received as a child before you cross the street, "stop, look and listen" then proceed.

Key Points

1) Don't have a serious conversation, or critique, right before someone is going to give a presentation, preach a sermon, or go to work. Although sometimes it is necessary, for the most part some conversations can wait. Wait until the person has completed their event, presentation, etc., and communicate any concerns, or critiques after the event.

2) Take the time to communicate empathetically and you will experience less stress, drama and conflict in your relationships.

3) Remember; don't have a serious conversation when you are tired. It's okay to say, *"you know, I want to give you the time you need and I want to be able to*

clearly understand—can we wait until tomorrow because I am exhausted?"

I know sometimes it can't be avoided so if you have to have a serious talk while you are tired, try to do more listening to avoid saying something you will later regret.

Now go and communicate effectively—you will feel so much better.

www.ingramcontent.com/pod-product-compliance
Lightning Source LLC
Chambersburg PA
CBHW071744040426
42446CB00012B/2469